Aquifers of Love

Also by Kimmy Sophia Brown

The Time Signature of Night: Poems

Works in Progress:

Sixty Second Thor

Zen Mothering: The Sound of One Head Pounding

Aquifers of Love

Poems

Kimmy Sophia Brown

World Community Press
Gray, Maine

© 2022 by Kimmy Sophia Brown
All Rights Reserved Worldwide

Published in 2022 in the United States of America
by the World Community Press, Gray, Maine 04039
worldcommunitypress.com

First paperback edition, 2022

This book takes advantage of modern, digital, print-on-demand technologies
and may, over time, be printed by more than one printer. If you receive a copy
that fails to meet our high expectations of quality, please inform us by emailing:

publishers@worldcommunitypress.com

You may reach the author at kimbrown@worldcommunity.com
if you wish to send her your remarks or feedback about this book.

Cover Image:
Promotional photo for the film *Through the Back Door* (1921)
with Mary Pickford, a sweet dog (name unknown), and the mule Maud.
With our appreciation to the Mary Pickford Foundation.

Hummingbird in Logo
Photo of an Allen's Hummingbird by Robin Rodvold

Photo of Kim, age six, taken by her Mom or Dad
Photo of Mama by Tymon Brown on her sixty-seventh birthday
("Holy sh*t, how did that happen!" KB)

Designed by the World Community Press

ISBN-13: 978-0-9635706-9-7 (paperback)

First Publication Date: October 28, 2022
Publication Edit Date: July 4, 2023

For my Mother and Father who loved and encouraged me.

Contents

POEMS

જી

Preface

My mother introduced me to poetry when I was a child. She loved Christina Rosetti and Edna St. Vincent Millay. I think I was eleven or twelve when she showed me "Patterns" by Amy Lowell, which shocked me to think that my mother could identify with passions like that!

Later while babysitting and watching late-night television I saw Rod McKuen recite his poem, "A Cat Named Sloopy." I was smitten with his free verse style and his voice. I think I was about fourteen.

I started keeping a journal when I was eleven, after reading *Harriet the Spy* by Louise Fitzhugh and *The Diary of Anne Frank*. Poems started coming to me, snippets here and there.

When I was fifteen I won First Prize from *American Girl Magazine* for the first poem I ever submitted anywhere: "And When I Die." For some reason winning shut me down with a strange terror!

Around the age of twenty, I acquired an anthology of English and American poems of the twentieth century, most of them written in the eras before and after WWI and WWII. I carried it with me in my suitcase during years of travel, and its contents comforted and inspired me.

I still journal most days, and that's usually when poems come.

We were compiling what we thought would be one book of poetry, but when it looked like it might become as gargantuan as *Leaves of Grass* or *The Faery Queen*, we decided to make two books.

What is the difference between them you might ask? While using the same alphabet, they are a pile of entirely different poems!

If there are two volumes, and you have both, you can carry one in each hand and be in perfect balance.

If there was only one massive volume and you tried to carry it, you might have a subluxation of the spine and thereby require a trip to the chiropractor or a Doctor of Osteopathy. Therefore, I felt responsible to prevent injuries to readers and divide them into two volumes. You're welcome!

The books have been waiting a lifetime to be born. The titles are *Aquifers of Love* and *The Time Signature of Night*. The poems in both books reflect the themes of the titles. The phrase "Aquifers of Love" expresses that there are countless places all around us where love can be found, both in the human experience and in nature.

"The Time Signature of Night" draws attention to the music that exists everywhere: the obvious music, such as birdsong and insect and animal sounds, but also the quieter music that is drowned out by our cerebral-heavy world. Dorothy Maclean of Findhorn wrote that every plant has a deva that sings it into being. Johannes Kepler wrote of the music of the spheres. We are living in a time of cosmic awakening when we can each finally hear the song of our soul.

My prayer is that our malformed culture will be transformed as we become aware of the inner power and beauty that we share with Gaia, our beautiful planet, and the universe. May the Divine Creator's love teach us and bless us all.

Kimmy Sophia Brown
Gray, Maine

Acknowledgments

I want to thank my dear husband, Peter, who worked with me for many hours on this book. I thank him for his encouragement and for his time editing and listening and suggesting and compiling and producing this for me. His help was precious and indispensable. Our love is deepening every day, thank you, sweetheart.

Thank you to Ruth Richmond, Betty Schniepp, and Mrs. Arons—mentors and teachers I had growing up.

Thank you to Surya Mitchell, Genevieve Lessard, and Maureen Spagnolo—friends with whom I shared many laughs and tears, as well as the creative process.

Thank you to Mary Angela Douglas, Claire Bowles, Larry Moffitt, and Nancy Oliver who have encouraged me and inspired me with their writing.

Thank you to Pam Moffatt for the eight years we spent doing *The Artist's Way* and Julia Cameron's subsequent books, striving to be each others' "believing eyes."

Thank you to my Women's Circle and all the ones who have been a part of it over the years, and who helped me find my voice again. Katey, Sarah, Wendy, Julie, Nikki, Lisa, Chris, Amanda, Lauren, and also Anna, Zizi, Anne, Anne-Marie, Erica, Bonny, the other Lisa, and the other Wendy. I love you all.

Thank you to my children: Tymon, Grace, Ranin, and Tadin who inspired me, made me laugh, made life such a joyful journey, and still do.

My love for you extends into the oxygen-starved strata of outer space, past the most mysterious and scariest and most beautiful gaseous photon belts of the universe, past where space squids dwell, and past that place where things fall off the edge of the universe. Past that. No, farther. Nope, keep going. Also deeper than the deepest taproot extending into the deepest mud among the darkest, squiggliest things at the deepest bottom of whatever is at the bottom of everything. Below that. Keep digging. Get a drill. Nope, keep going.

Thank you to my parents, Fen and Iris Korman, who encouraged and loved me. I want to go buy soft ice cream cones with you again and sit at a picnic table in the sun and laugh together while they melt down our wrists into our sleeves. I miss you more than I can say!

I thank every person, every dog, cat, horse, cow, sheep, goat, pig, squirrel, chipmunk, vole, mole, dragonfly, mouse, whale, dolphin, jellyfish, roly-poly, bird, tree, flower, weed, vegetable, mineral, and stink bug I ever met or saw, and everything and everyone else too. I love you all.

I thank the most gracious and loving unseen helpers, the nature spirits and fairies, and the beautiful, sweet, divine Creator who thought of everything first.

Miracles occur naturally as expressions of love.
The real miracle is the love that inspires them.
In this sense, everything that comes from love is
a miracle.[1]

"The Meaning of Miracles: #3"
in *A Course in Miracles*

Amor saca amor.

(Love begets love.)[2]

Teresa of Avila

Poems

Aquifers of Love

When I realized I didn't know everything
I could abandon my opinions.

This pathway is a long, blind curve.
Some noisy travelers
obscure the path
as they beat their confident drums.

We need silence
to find the sacred light within.

It is not ostentatious—
It throws quiet shadows on the walls.

It says
Hush.
You know what to do.
No one can tell you.

Listen for the sound of underground waters.
Aquifers of love.

Eclipse

My dear friend called she said We drove to Idaho for the eclipse we camped it was the most amazing thing a black hole in the sky in the middle of the day we saw the stars the weird light it was beautiful the most incredible experience of my life I cried and cried

I thought about that day I was not in the direct line of the event I cooked food and drove a car for repair I kind of looked up when the light on the trees got eerie and strange I didn't pay attention I was busy

She said it was glorious even holy

I thought how often I miss things because I'm not paying attention To see the stars in the daytime To notice I am on a planet in space Now Today Miracles all around me Holy holy holy

Tranquility Seems to Beckon

From the thrashing jowls
of insomnia
I rise at three
for tea and toast
and finally steal
to the sofa,
where tranquility
seems to beckon.

Until
the
chuckling
genii
of
a
dog
fart
finds
its
way
up
my
nose.

Eyes

I've known eyes,
large, open,
and
relaxed,
that shut and squint
over time.
Maybe too much sun
or too much pain.

I've heard our eyes
are the same
from birth.
That may be so
but the collective clobbers
of a lifetime
can create a wince-reaction
that tightens
these dreamy
liquid
colored
spheres,
that reveal
the mysteries
of the soul—
the waking hours
and the dreams.

What is a cataract
maybe it is the eye
saying
I can't bear
to see
any
more.

There's a Dream in My Bed

My little son woke me and whispered,
"There's a dream in my bed."
He crawled in beside me.
"Will you be with me and keep me safe?"

The shadowy house creaked,
the furnace roared,
the cats chased,
we went to sleep.

Soon I heard his congested breathing
as his little arm fell against me.
I prayed for his sweet, young life,
that he would always feel encircled by my love.

The Intelligence of Children

Freud said the intelligence of children
outshines the dullness of adults.

They are open to beauty,
kindness,
the obvious truths—
unfettered by darkness.

They speak in the language
between languages,
they take in signs.
They have senses that
translate languageless realms.

They grasp generosities
lost to impervious adults.
Maybe that's why God
starts us over and over
with new babies
until we get it.

How do we get it?

I Cried When We Took
Our Old TV to Goodwill

I cried when we took our old TV to Goodwill.
I kept rubbing its forehead, thanking it.
Apologizing.
It felt like leaving a kid at the orphanage.

What is that?
Old barns, old houses call to me,
their longing and abandonment
catch my eye like a neglected dog.

Once when I was a kid,
I threw my bike down in anger.
Then, flooded with remorse
I knew I was supposed
to be kind and love everything.
It was like a whispered secret.

Your rocking chair
doesn't have a pulse,
but it does.
A wristwatch, a television, a cup.
The vibration of love is everywhere.
Gratitude thaws indifference.
Science may tell you
your teddy bear is not alive.
But who cares?

Someday,
if you notice your toaster
beaming at you with adoration,
pat its head, make some toast,
and smile back.

God On the Pillow

God lays his head on the pillow
next to me and we talk.
As soon as I begin
to tell him everything
I can feel his response.

I know what I did wrong
I know what I should do better
I know what I have to fix

When God is in bed with me
I know where I'm going.

My sincerest self
surges to the surface
and all I want to do
is forgive myself
and everyone else.

I thank him for the pilot light of love
that burns within me.
Let it roar.

Sun-Flecked Drive

In my sun-flecked drive to work
I said I love you to a mailbox with
hand-painted flowers,
an orchard
happy with new apples,
a work-worn wooden cart, and
a field-tired tractor.
I prayed for people
randomly.
The guy in the red car,
the folks
in the darkened house.
I thought of Yogananda
lighting his smile of smiles.
I smiled all the way
to work,
and the light lessened my
private torments.

The Death of a Mouse

Why must a tiny life die such a scary death?
The cat presented
the delicate body.
She lay on the floor with her large flannel-soft ears
and tiny frame,
prone and delicate.
I thought she was dead.
But she must have been resting.

The cat suddenly
pounced and chased,
and they were gone.
I hadn't seen her tiny chest rising and falling,
so very tired.

Leaving for work in the morning,
the cat was staked out,
waiting for her to make a move.
He wanted sympathy and breakfast,
after watching all night.

All I could think of was
this tiny injured being
hiding under the refrigerator in fear,
probably dying,
until
she finally passes
through the mousehole in the sky
where there are no cats
and no traps.
Enough food
for her entire family,
all the generations
before her
and those to come.

The History of Real Estate

I loved my tree-sheltered childhood home.
The oak canopies and maple sentries.
Maple keys and acorns
in my sandbox under the swing set.
Thickets of lilacs
mingled roots and fragrance
with lilies of the valley.
Fir and spruce
too sticky to climb
rubbed elbows
with mountain ash and apple.
We played beneath their skirts.
Cops n robbers.
Pioneers.
Hide n seek.
The trees played too,
breathing slow
and standing still.

Then we moved away.

Decades later,

Google Earth!
The joyous rocket of reunion!
I saw my house exposed
like a naked prisoner.

The turf picked clean,
scavenged to the bone.
Not a single tree standing.

My grief. A lump
I can not swallow.

Prior to the Cold River Plunge Fully Clothed

Oh, hesitation.
You hold me back in practicality
when the wee one within would gladly
splash in mud
but oh,
calculation.

I'll be wet and dirty,
says my maturity.
But I refuse to get old and dignified
with my hair styled and blow-dried,
so I leap in the current
and soon, the deterrent
becomes my pleasure,
what fun!
So much for sophistication.

Santa Cruz 1973

Four giggling, goofy girls
after a shrieking thrill
on the rickety roller coaster,
walked along the moonlit coast road home.
Seized by a loony inspiration,
we climbed down the cliffs,
bounded across the empty beach,
stripped off our clothes,
and plunged into the freezing Pacific.
Snort-laughing and screaming,
wet and sand encrusted,
we ran home
where we
warmed flour tortillas
on the gas jet
and ate them
with butter.
Still dripping,
laughing, and
loving being eighteen.

[for Genevieve, Beth, and Karen]

Tree Gal

Tall trees
call me
bless me
make me cry.
Feel bark
leaf heart
eye to eye.

Ephemerons

How long should I keep things?
Five birds' nests on my bookcase,
three turtle shells,
a paper wasp's nest,
so many sea shells.

Two thousand books
murmuring their author's hearts.
A tub of a hundred journals.
A thousand old letters
and uncatalogued photos.
These are my nests.
These are my shells.
I'll live with them
till I depart too.

Pirate's Breakfast

On pancake day,
the lusty forks
traverse the syrup sea.
Golden bullion
stacked on plates
in siren songs
say "Bite me."
The eyelids sink,
the bellies grow,
indulgence of the dumb.
Sing Yo Ho Ho for coffee,
to go with a bottle of rum.

Loving Everybody

I have loved so many people.
I can see their faces in my mind.
Of course, God has loved everyone ever born
beyond my little loving.
Sometimes I can relate to that.

I see faces passing on the street,
or think of the people I know.
I feel so driven to love.

I wonder, is there anyone I really can't love?
It seems so easy in general.
But
in particular
is where it gets hard.

The Little Ones

You who created
Divine Love
please guide us.

We weep for the little ones
who cried out for you,
misused by
the Trusted Ones.

Pitiless tormenters
dispensing
confusion
in secrecy.
Wafers and wine
and unchecked suffering.

The guilty wear their robes.
Everything is fine.
People can't believe it.
They don't want to know.

After the Farm

Stirring me stirring me stirring me
the things that lie sleeping inside.
Skeletons rise and soulful searching
awaken to things once denied.
Original God, original me
I wonder where lies the connection?
So many born on the face of the earth
looking for honest direction.
Lie in our beds
with tears on our cheeks
streaking our pillows and souls.
Fragmented fractional partial and split.
So many halves, looking for wholes.

[lyrics looking for a tune]

Like a Clamshell

Openness and trust
are like two sides of a clamshell.
I clamp tight
because I don't like trespassers.
People can be like paparazzi,
snapping pictures,
snapping judgments,
skimming the top.
If only that "do unto others"
thing was the norm.
I'd open like a clamshell
on a steamer.

You Can Hear the Ocean

I might have been three
the first time I knew magic was real.
Someone held a conch shell to my ear and said,
See? You can hear the ocean.
I heard it
and was smitten
with the mystery of it all.
Even though the factual and the logical
tried to dissuade me,
I never looked back.

Forgiveness

Dr. Cross.
His nurse, Myra.
My parents.

I am three.
In the examination room with

Dr. Cross!
His nurse, Myra!
My parents!

They turn me over to give me a shot.
They all hold me down.
I fight with all my strength,
kicking and screaming.
The needle goes in my butt cheek,
I scream.
The adults laugh.
I want to kill them.
I am seething, furious, shamed, betrayed.
In that weird place where adults think
you won't remember.

They had to do it.
It was for my own good.
I stand on the table,
I rage at them.
They laugh.
I will never forget it.

Dr. Cross.
His nurse, Myra.
My parents.

Great Uncle Tony

My father's family
were printers.
I never knew them.
Just a visit to
Great Uncle Tony's house
when I was small.

His overstuffed barn,
cobwebby and chaotic,
was littered with
chairs and tools.
I was startled
by a turtle shell
as big as a saddle.

He and Aunt Gert
had a bowl of
butterscotch candies.
I loved them.
All of them.

Later,
a psychic told me
she saw a man
showing me
his inky fingers.

Uncle Tony?

The psychic
couldn't say.

I wondered if he brought me
a butterscotch.

My Mom the Bird Lady

People brought fledglings to my mom,
the ad hoc wildlife queen.
Making nests with kleenex,
she warmed them
in her hands,
and in their pleading throats
fed them
canned dog food
with a straw.

Some didn't make it.
Some became family members:
Junior Jones, the robin
Charlie Brown, the grackle
Pip Squeak, the red squirrel.

Her advice to
well-meaning saviors:

Leave them alone.
Their mother is watching.
But if in real danger
save them.
Human touch
does not deter
the mother-baby bond.

She was a disciple
of Rachel Carson.
A vigil keeper, protector.
weeper, defender.

Nod to Will Rogers:
She never met an animal
she didn't like.

Whale Rider

In the dark theater
wrappers rustle,
ice slushes in the echo of wax cups,
the air conditioning
blows like arctic air,
agony on bare knees
and sandaled feet.

On the screen,
the Maori girl presses her nose
against the forehead of the whale,
and in the dark of the gray morning
climbs the barnacles onto his back.

The blowhole erupts
and the huge rudder
slaps awake.
The girl rides the back of the whale
with her ancestors,
until she's underwater
and lets go.

I look at my daughter
on one side of me.
Her eyes are wet.
At my husband,
and his are too.
We look at the screen
and we cry with the whale,
the girl,
and her tribe.

The world is waiting
for the One who is to come.
But, it's all of us who are to come.

I like movies better than church.
I find God on the screen.
He grabs my heart
and we cry together
in the dark popcorn sanctuary.

Your Large Soft Eye

My crazed and wounded inner Ahab
has spent a lifetime pursuing You,
elusive as the White Whale.
Lowering and launching the boats of my prayers,
which have dragged and dashed
through the squalls of my life.

For all of my longing,
it could be that I was in Your belly
all this time.
The bars were not a prison,
but your ribs surrounding me.
What I thought was my own heart
was Yours beating with mine.

I could never harpoon you,
never spill blood,
I will search for the spout of your spirit
on the horizon of prayer.

Am I in my own way?
I have no thought to harm You or anyone,
but the years of struggle
have made a crazy impulse
to jump from the crow's nest.

As I sink in the deep water,
I want to glimpse your large, soft eye,
reflecting the sun overhead.
I hope that our eyes
recognize each other
for a moment,
and rest there,
before I pass.

My Monster

I'm feeling
particularly sad today.
I let my monster out.
She screamed
and raged.
Justified,
exasperated.

Should I feed her?
When I starve her,
she gets quiet,
but she's always there,
growling,
tethered
in the basement.

She doesn't know
where she came from.
She just is.
She wants to be heard,
loved,
seen.

If she was,
she might settle down
for a nice big lick,
a loud purr,
a long nap.

The basement is dark.
It's been so long since
she's been let out
that when a crack of light comes in
she goes bonkers.

Pulling at the wall
till the chain breaks,
she runs around and howls,
scratching things.

She knocks over lamps
breaks door jams,
and behaves in a way
that most people
DO
NOT
LIKE.

She could behave—
maybe.
Should I put her down?
She's dangerous,
but doesn't think she is.

She can be
a very nice monster,
but has been known
to breathe fire
and vaporize the guests.

If she finds out
that no one wants her,

she'll terrorize the village
and eat everyone.

I have a plan.
I'm going to send her
down the path.
There's a big sign:

This way to the Party!
Monsters Welcome!

She'll run toward it,
so excited.

There's a cliff behind the sign.
She'll fall down
and down and down
in the dark crevasse.

She'll be confused.

Where the party hats?
Where the cake?
It dark in here.

Dark, dark, dark.

No party.
Cry.
Mad.
Roar.
Eat everyone.

Falling, falling.
Dark. See nothing.
Cold air.
Falling.

Thinking . . .
Alone.
Where everybody?
Cry more.

When monsters cry,
get out of the way.
Tears as big as
swimming pools,
sticky, voluminous
snot.

Liars!
Ditched!
Alone!
Falling.
No bottom.

An open crack in the universe.

She cries herself to sleep.

When she wakes up,
she's lying on warm sand
by the ocean.

She's not a monster
anymore.

Just a person
with holes in her soul,
trying to figure out this
thing
called
life.

My Terrible Toes

My terrible toes
marched
on the front line.
They stand in formation
like broken-down soldiers.
Never AWOL.

Not one bolted
to try and find herself,
hitchhiking to places
where she could walk
alone on warm sand.

Being a toe
is like being a
conjoined twin.
Never alone.
Always in a pack.

That one big toe
has been odd
for a long time.
The others
don't like her.

"If we don't look at her,
we can pretend
she's not with us."

My toes are not ballerinas.
They are po-ta-toes.

They carry the load of Me.
Another day?
Yes ma'am! Ten-Hut!
One two, one two,
stomp stomp stomp.

Nail polish would be like
putting hippos in tutus.

Some folks earn a Purple Heart.
I was awarded the Purple Toe.

Someday I'd Like to Be Small

Someday I'd like to be small.
With a little body a man could easily carry.
Small hands and feet.
Pretty dresses, pretty hair
and people would say
"She's a lovely little thing,"
and they would mean
Me.

The Mystery of Matter

I've always been a big girl,
but once I knew this handsome boy
from Nicaragua
who was my buddy.
He loved to carry me around
and when I started laughing,
my atoms became lighter.
In the midst of giddy giggling
we stumbled on a secret!
The science of matter
or anti-matter
is hidden in a laugh.

Love Is the Densest Bone

Does love conquer all?
What do you think?
Love is light.
Love is water.
Everything is made of love
and we are light and water.

When all is torn from you,
boiled away to the grounds,
nothing left but light and water
on this firmament,

and faith seems silly,
and plans are worse—

then love is the densest bone.

Confession

It was me.
When I visited.
I'm talking about
the finger tracing
through the frosting
at the base of the chocolate cake
in the fridge.
You scolded your kids.
But it was me.
What a relief that's off my chest—
a burden I've carried over fifty years!

Going in Peace

I go to the forest
to the pine cathedral
to a little wooden house
with sawdust in the hole,
and a crescent moon on the door,
where I can go in peace.

Full Moon Cat

While the full moon shone down last night,
our cat staged a private Olympics.
From my bed,
I heard him downstairs
throwing the shot put and the javelin.
He sprinted up the stairs and
shoved his whiskers in my face.

Then he conducted his weekly rodent pogrom.

Finally,
he hauled out his Harry Belafonte records
and danced until the Day-O.

Around then, my alarm went off.
Clutching my coffee,
I passed him curled on the sofa,
lifting an eyelid as if to say,
"What's yer problem?"

The Rooster

The song of a soul is a funny thing.
The rooster up the road crows
fifty times a day.
He sounds exactly the same every time.
He is happy to tell us
that the sun is up at 3 a.m.
when it is still dark
or at noon when it is raining.

He never seems embarrassed about it, like:
"Maybe I already told them," or
"Maybe I'm too loud."

He never starts and stops mid-crow
as if he lost his mojo.
He was born with that song in his heart
and he gives it his all every time.

All You Can Eat
Roadside Buffet

Look at that open field,
the thigh-high cacophony of
yarrow and milkweed,
Queen Anne's lace and clover,
black-eyed Susans and St John's wort,
spiny elbows by elbows,
filmy colored wings by wings,
pokey proddy pointy antennas by antennas.
Dragonflies, butterflies, bees,
and what have you,
proboscises poised and probing,
slurping up nectar and pollen,
every sort of insect-loving yum
in the late summer throb and buzz
of crickets and grasshoppers
alighting on yellows and reds—
a humming holiday of late summer.

Someone thought mowing was a good idea.
The desecration of this fine feast,
everything cut and dry,
why?
Why?

Breakfast

There is no sound
of teeth on bread.
It does not satisfy.
But the crunch of toast
evokes!
A potbellied mug of coffee
enjoyed while butter soaks.
If I were far away
somewhere
cold with rain and snow
I'd conjure out of empty air
this comfort food of home.

Ode to Garlic

Oh, you Goddess!
You temptress!
Everything you touch
turns fragrant
and exotic.

Smooth and white,
hard and supple,
clothed in layers
of gauzy lace,
that fall away
exposing flawless skin.

You cut through haze,
make bland exciting.
Elusive.
Penetrating.
You take my breath away.

And everyone else's too!

The Last Egg

I'm waiting . . .
going from window to window
door to door.
Front door back door
cupboard door refrigerator door.
Mailman brings bills
four-color catalogs
stuff we'll never buy.

We've got the last egg
the last potato
a jar of mustard
plenty of salt
(so I won't need to look back).

Pacing all over the house
nothing to sell
nowhere to work
heart beating
lungs breathing
books waiting to be read
utilities waiting to be turned off
one by one.
Like little deaths.
No phone
no electricity
no water
no food
no house
but still alive.

And they wonder why people write
Bad Checks.

Water

Dirty laundry needs to soak
aquifers serve pine and oak
wild herds a water hole
domestic pets their water bowl.

Droughts cause mass evaporation
rains bring relief and rehydration.
When fields and farms
are cracked and dry
folks pray for rain so crops won't die.

Jesus turned water into wine
because to thirst is human,
to quench, divine.

Palm Sunday

On Palm Sunday, everyone remembers
how Jesus rode into Jerusalem
on a donkey.
The people waved palm branches,
and we still pass them out in church
before Easter.
No-one remembers the donkey.
Was she tired when she arrived,
was she spooked by the crowds?
Did she bray or balk?
Did he coax her with soft sounds?
Most days, she was loaded with burdens,
but he was different.
He didn't scold or beat her,
he touched her ears kindly,
sang to her,
fed her some grapes.
At the watering trough
while she drank,
he rubbed her neck
and looked into her smoky eyes.
She was just a borrowed donkey
but she served someone who saw her soul.

Little Chirping Songbird

While I'm still under my blankets
and the light of dawn shines under
the edge of the shade,
I feel that old ocean liner of sadness
sliding in,
trying to dock in my harbor.
He's so familiar, this huge black beast,
I nearly throw back the covers and invite him in.
"Oh well, why not,
I've known you all my life."

But then this little chirping songbird shows up
like a cartoon bird from a Disney movie,
singing away in my ear,

"No No, you can choose gratitude today,
you can choose joy!" it insists.

And I realize it's true.
Then the black beast withdraws
like a cloud overtaken by the sun.

Driving a Truck

In my truck, the other trucks seem friendly.
Like beasts lumbering
in recognition of their breed,
nosing one another like elephants.
The highway affinity.
Toll booth smiles.
Girl truckers, boy truckers
astride diesel pumps,
conscious of their massive dominion
over the roads,
swaggering.
Bumping along in a caravan
like Bedouins of the desert,
sheiks on camels,
turbaned rajahs on elephants.
No coconuts at this oasis.
Coffee and eggs over light.

Starving Artist
on Kinnikkinnick

In Milwaukee, the winter of 1977 was
a freeze of uncompromising darkness.
I ate in the weird little cosmos of
George Webb's greasy-spoon establishments—
on a par
with White Castle.
No, swanky, compared to White Castle.

They catered to people with no money.
You could get a burger
or eggs really cheap,
and free refills on coffee.

Once I was sitting in a miserable state of mind,
but I said a quiet Grace before my plate.
A man saw me pray—he paid for my food.
I was blown away with gratitude
because it meant
that I had two more dollars
to go toward my next meal.

In those days,
I sang "The Boxer"
because I understood
"seeking out the poorer quarters
where the ragged people go."

Kinnickkinnick is a street in Milwaukee.
The definition is a smoking mixture used by
North American Indians as a substitute for tobacco
or for mixing with it, typically consisting of
dried sumac leaves and the inner bark
of willow or dogwood.

"The Boxer" is a song written by Paul Simon.

Does the Earth Purr
When It Rains?

Does the earth purr when it rains?
This limbless being
covered with earthlings,
mites of all sizes and shapes
biting and scratching,
leaving gouges and holes,
erecting scaffolding and scarring her hide—

Does anyone lie in the grass
and murmur words of love?
Does anyone caress her skin,
run fingers through her seaweed?
Do we groom her for her pleasure?
The rain must be soothing.
I want to put my ear on the throat of the earth
and hear her purr.

If Bees Pollinate
in the Key of C

If bees pollinate in the key of C
what is the key of a stinging hornet?
In fact, is the entire cosmos annotated?
When Johannes Kepler heard
the music of the spheres,
was his ear tilted up, cheek on palm,
smiling like the Mona Lisa,
listening to the enormous roar of the planets?
Listening in his body,
the way notes vibrated Beethoven's floor as he lay
under the piano banging chords?
Did Johannes
notate the cosmic vibrations
in galactic shorthand,
attempting to record the song of the expanding Milky Way
and the songs of the planets—
millions
turning whirring spinning singing
in a truly mesmerizing Hallelujah chorus,
of a most coordinated miracle of a WILD NOW,
defying place and time—
convoluted and inverted
and too big to map or conceive or understand or cognize
except for a humble mumble of
"My father and mother who art in heaven
please teach me
my part
in this miraculous song
of overwhelm."

A Glass of Cardinal Song

There's nothing new about
being drunk on fragrance,
but I wonder,
as I stand beneath
the heavy lilac blossoms,
if I shouldn't drive today,
or operate heavy machinery.

If they forced a breathalyzer test,
the reading would say
Too much lilac in the blood.

I'm in an altered state.
Slurring words,
staggering,
the truth serum of nature
taking effect.
I'm blurting out whatever I think.
This fragrance fills my head.

Am I a danger to myself
and others?

Perhaps a lie-down on the lawn would help,
but now I hear the singing birds.

Oh God!

A glass of cardinal song,
of robin.

I'm done in.

I must lie under these clouds and sleep it off
until the stars come out.

When I awake, I want to drink of those as well,
and the thrush, and the crickets.

Really, God, You are the greatest bartender.

Set 'em up. Put 'em on my tab.

Vegetable Spa

Come here, my little garlic clove
white as a tiny tusk.
I'll massage you in my kitchen
for it is almost dusk.
The pan is on the burner
the broccoli's in the steam
the butter waits for garlic
the garlic waits for cream.
Cardamom seeds are popping
the eggplant looks mysterious
turmeric and cumin
make the kitchen smell delirious.
Come back, my little cauliflower,
let me lull you with my story.
Come for a swim with all your friends
in a bath of seasoned curry.

Buzzards' Breakfast

The winter cornfield.
Dry as an old man's shins.
A dozen buzzards congregate
around an unfortunate carcass.

Wings are flapping
as they chew the fat.
The only thing missing
is a coffee pot.

The Gnat and I

A glance into my Pinot Noir,
a tiny being swimming,
with finger tip I fish him out
(his intention to be winging).
He sits upon my digit warm—
legs mopping wine from wings.
After drying sufficiently,
flies off to other things.

Lead Her Off the Bench

I am dowsing every day for the
water of Your love,
feeling tugs on the branches
of my being.
Nudges that tell me
I have wandered
into desert or
that water is nigh.
When my mind is clear,
Your divinity
is everywhere.
When my awareness wanes,
my inner judge pounds her gavel madly,
gleefully dispensing verdicts.

I want to quietly lead her off the bench,
remove the black robe,
and push her off the dock.

Because she needs a swim
in Your shining water.

My Office Is a Baked Potato

My office is painted
White and
Filtered Sunlight.
My leather chair is
pale as new butter.

My room is a
salted
buttered
baked
potato.

I wear a spud-colored
Irish sweater
in the soft yellow
lamplight.

I dig up thoughts.
White potato-meat poems,
winter thoughts,
soft thoughts,
bare-tree thoughts.

The trees'
burnt bronzey
Tahitian-tan leaves
are now a potato-chip-crisp carpet,
orange-crush,
crunching brown boots bearing
down on Cheetos
and Cheerios.

Outside,
all the lush summer greens
have stiffened
in jarring air and
hard ground.

The hot-air furnace roars.
My old
creamsicle dog
smiles and
groans
moving
her rusty joints.

The oven beeps.
The pie
burned a bit,
its baked
brown crust
charred.

We crunch the crust.
Warm pie melts
into our bones,
orangey, squashy,
pumpkiny
in the ovens
of our bodies.

Sometimes I Forget
My Sense of Humor

Jiminy Cricket!
Sometimes
I forget my sense of humor.
How can that be?
In high school
my best friend Gen and I said,
"The purpose of life is to laugh!"
And we did.
We laughed our asses off.
About everything.
We called her glaring judgmental father
Glarry.
We projected lewd meanings onto Christmas carols:
It Came Upon a Midnight Clear,
and laughed our hineys off some more.

Throughout my adult life
I breathed ironic comments
to fellow underlings,
as the person in charge
pontificated
while we giggled.

Through the zany years
of being around my four hilarious children
I found myself chuckling
as Tymon's monkey voice warned us of
"Fire and brimstone!"

All I can say is
if the world goes to hell in a handbasket
it damn well better pack a joke book for the ride
or I ain't getting in.
You can give my ticket to some wet blanket
who forgot how to laugh.

The Day After
I Didn't Kill Myself

The day after I didn't kill myself,
the sun came out.
The dark, hopeless mood shifted.
Nothing lasts forever.
The wall I thought was blocking me
dissipated.
Moods are like weather.
Rain rains, but when it's through
something else comes.
My death will come someday—
sure enough—
but I don't have to help it
with self-violence.
I can watch my kitten tip over
my wastebasket.
Listen to a five-year-old girl sing
"Fly Me to the Moon" on YouTube.
Smell flowers over a fence.
And let my factory-installed heart
keep ticking,
happy that it lived.

The Second Day After
I Didn't Kill Myself

On the second day after I didn't kill myself
the sun was still shining
and though
the great black mood
was still there a little,
the light got in somehow
and I was glad I was still here.

What is this life force
that burns in us?
So strongly in some?
The caged animal,
the refugee,
the prisoner.

Why does the light
dance in some hearts?
And some hearts give up?

God, help me desire life
as long as I have it.
Let me live it
as long as it is given me.

Emergence

For years I lived in a
pile of stones.
My body felt like a boulder,
detached from my thoughts
and soul.

There are unseen forms
that reside in granite
until the sculptor's tools
reveal them.

I feel crumbles,
hear cracks
in the granite of my former self.

Shedding what no longer serves me
I wake up,
finding
the precious unhatched eggs
of the tiny birds
of my dreams,
who will very soon
peck free
from their shells
and fly.

The Storage Cellar

In my storage cellar are my jars of pain.

Pickled stories of resentment.
A still-born baby of a broken dream.
Swallowed pride,
tangled hurt.

Lost love goes on the back of the bottom shelf.

Self-pity has a broken seal,
leaking out a stinky vapor.

Rage is hard to bottle.
It's all over the wall.

But see those little flowers
growing in the dirt?
They're from seeds of kindness
someone dropped.

Most of the stuff in here is past expiration.

If I compost it all,
something new and gorgeous
can blossom
for sure.

Call My Me!

I call my me!
Who are me?
Who am me?
Walking in the green air
of the wet woods
so silent.
I want to hear
and see.
To be
my me
with Thee.

What Is My Weather?

What is my weather?
Sometimes
I attract clouds

        storms
        lightning.

But I prefer the gentle light of morning
that nudges birds awake
that beckons flowers open
that bathes the cat yawning and stretching
in a swatch of yellow sun.

The mother touch of morning
is where I wish to live.

I Didn't Get the Deluxe Set

It's a good thing
that I wasn't born
looking like
Marilyn Monroe.
I wouldn't have known
how to carry all that stuff
around with me.
It must take special skills
to have that face and body
and deal with everybody
wherever you go.
It's a good thing
I didn't get the deluxe set.
Phew.

Mining for God

I sit in the riverbed
sifting sand
sifting sand
the glint of gold has been mined away.

I've got my pointy hammer,
knocking on the rock walls,
chipping off chunks,
feeling my way,
looking for that mother lode
where You are.

But you are dust too,
and rock,
yes?
The chipping, the pounding, the search,
it's all one, isn't it?

Prayers are not just "blessed be's."
They are coughing and choking in the dark,
lighting match after match blown out in the wind.

They are the continuing,
feeling for the wall,
and for firm footing.
It's all gold, isn't it?

Some Women Are . . .

Some women are egrets.
Unbearably graceful,
long necks,
reed-thin legs,
dignified bearing.
They glide and float,
personifying elegance.
All who see them
cannot look away.

Some women are flowers.
Fragrant, flowing, fragile,
petal-like faces
that open and close,
bending and blowing in wind and rain.
Beaming in the sun,
breathtaking and bonny.

Some women are root vegetables.
Rutabagas. Round, rough, red.
Strong, long, roots embedded
in cold, dark earth.
Potato women.
Mashable, bakeable, roastable.
Delicious.
Women like turnips and parsnips and carrots,
crunchy and thick as clubs,
fresh in a cold winter cellar.

But when these women bake!
They're the softest
and the hottest.
They melt
the coldest butter
or the coldest heart.

Talking with God in My Pajamas

If I sit like this,
If I say these words
in this way,
If I kneel and bow,
If I repeat this text,
If I genuflect . . .
If? If?
This was the confusion
of You and Me,
my whole life.

How do I become "acceptable"?
"Worthy"?

What I really want to do
is to sit in an armchair
in my pajamas
and sip coffee while we talk.

Divine You, I say,
What do you think about life,
. . . about me?

How can I best be of service,
or at least
how can I do no harm?

I have no robes,
no altars that are more holy
than my kitchen table.

I find you in the groan of my old dog
when she lies down,
and in the snap yellow of the new autumn sun.

This to me seems normal.
Like the Purloined Letter,
I find You've been
here all along.

Make Love the Bubble in My Level

I prayed to God:

Make
love
the bubble in my level.

So wherever I am
I find
the median point,
and I can
fill holes
with the putty of love.

Replace rot
with hardwood beams
of love.

Foundations
of love
built to last.

Tiny Boy in July

Milk drunk eyes, blinking, sinking,
my tiny tummy kisses
make him fairly flinch.
But so sleepy sinking softly,
the tickly touch of kisses
rouse a smile and a twitch.
Then the lull of sleep is tingling
and he drifts and drifting sinking,
like a floating fairy feather,
and dreams like dreamy babies
of milk drinking in warm weather.

Hologram Dream

I had a dream.
My kids are small.
Tadin is seven,
searching for a lost toy.
Tymon has a computer.
Ranin has action figures.
Gracie opens the refrigerator
and says, "Mom, these bagels are moldy,"
and she throws them away.

I wake up and know
they're all adults,
and yet they're all the ages they've ever been to me:
newborn, toddler, child, adolescent, adult.

I was there for all of it.

When one of them was sixteen,
I asked someone we were visiting,
"Can he use the bathroom?"

I've committed all the parental faux pas
that make children die inside.
They have all cringed, but still.
But STILL.

They are my holy garden.
Watching them grow is the joy of my life.
And what fine pumpkins they are,
what fine sunflowers.
Their souls are huge and green.
What fine star seeds they are.
Magnificent humans.
See how they
SHINE AND SHINE.

Six-Week-Old Boy

I awake to the snuffling nose and coughing
of my six-week-old boy.
I am so tired,
delirious with loss of sleep
but I snap myself awake,
and scoop up the chubby curve of baby,
who grins and sucks,
milk spilling from his mouth corners.
We both soften to goo.
Then fed and belly down
I rub his little back.
He sighs and sputters,
tiny bottom
freshly diapered,
I stroke him into baby snores.

Mammals' Motherhood

Pregnant, attempting a nap,
groggy as a hibernating bear,
My cubs tumble over me.
Diapered bottoms roll across my face.
Shrieks
giggles
drool.
I resist only the worst of it,
with an occasional cuff or growl.
Mostly, I'm laughing too.

I glimpse their chubby faces
as they dive and wrestle.
Waiting for my third birth,
I feel linked to other mammals' motherhood.

I groan and grin,
receiving their little leaping bodies
wondering
how a mother leopard survives a litter.

Kids On the Lawn

The magnolia bloomed today,
the daffodils burst skyward.
Kids are playing in the twilight
on damp, spring lawns.
Red-faced and bright,
spring air fills their lungs.
Reluctant for supper and bedtime.

They throw themselves
into wild tumbling and races.
They come to the door for water,
and then launch themselves
back into the fray.

When it's too dark to see,
four scuffle through the door
into my arms.
Their hair smells like grass,
mud, and evening air.

Cool and sweaty,
hair in a tangle,
jeans stained with mud,
they exude the tonic
of children.

The bath is frothy.
They scorn it at first,
but then,
with rubber sharks,
dive in and attack.

Kitchen Billiards

I chalk the end of my mop
and pop
that watermelon chunk off the baseboard.
Look at the lineup on the floor:
a puddle of sticky apple juice,
a variety of crumbs,
a bacterial homestead.
I press against the table and take aim at stray toys
and lob them into the next room
with a vengeance.
I clean up that green-felt linoleum
like Minnesota Fats,
gather my winnings,
and flick off the light.

Marriage Like Apollo 13

If someone said:

"Your marriage is like Apollo 13.
You need to gather the duct tape,
the plastic bags,
all the tools, to make a carbon-scrubbing machine
to clean the oxygen of your love so you can survive,"

you would crawl into the compartment that is too small,
and let the part that blew up fall away.
You still might blow yourselves to smithereens,
but you also might
find your way back,
shaking and burning
through the atmosphere,
shaking your teeth loose,
hanging on to what's left of the ship.

What a lesson then,
learning to use what we have
instead of what we wish we had,
making it all work into a functioning thing,
and making landfall in one piece.

And in that joy of using everything we've got
to keep the ship going,
we realize to abandon it means we lose it all,
and that is a death we won't accept.

We're so glad we kept talking with Houston.
Is that one of God's names?

Spooky Action

When beings are connected
by blood
or love
and are separated by great distances
or circumstances,
the pull of their parts
send signals
through vast spaces
or maybe universes,
and finally
the great coincidences,
the great synchronicities
complete their orbit.

The migration of lost parts
complete their journey.
Sometimes
it results
in ecstatic joy
or choking sobs
or both.

"In quantum physics, entangled particles
remain connected so that actions performed on one
affect the other, even when separated by great distances.
The phenomenon so riled Albert Einstein he called it
'spooky action at a distance.'"[1]

The Secret of Sleep

There is a sleeping dance at my age,
the beeping of a bladder alarm
or waking in the chokehold of a bad dream.
My eyes are open, but I see nothing.
An occasional weird face that I blink away.
I roll over and try to
picture a View-Master blue sky with 3D white clouds,
but the bank account haunts me, the want of a job I love,
the desire to work out the knots in the wood of love.
Thoughts twirl like dandelion seeds
in a windy mind.
I wish I knew the secret of sleep.

Then the Thumping Starts

Ghoulish numbers on the clock.
3 a.m.
I sigh.
Farewell, sleep.
Finding slippers,
I shuffle past
sleeping spouse,
squeaking floorboards,
whining hinge,
and then
the thumping starts.

Sprawled like a tart on vacation
I find you on a couch.
"Silly goose! Let the belly rubs begin!"

Frenzied wags,
as if it's been months.
My cheek on your unbearably soft muzzle,
your sleepy eyes looking into mine,
your tail beating the crap out of the couch,
and I think,
how sweet you are, My Silly Goose.
I'm so glad.
Of all the biscuit joints in the world,
you came into mine.

Sweet Sorrel

The sorrel look like little clovers,
little shamrocks,
sweet and earnest.
Their little, green, threesome leaves
on short stems
fill in where the ground is dry.
Their tiny yellow flowers
fold shut in the chill.

They look proud.
They only took a month or so
from the tiniest nothing-looking seeds
to their great sprawling families—
like faithful little Catholics
smiling at Mary,
filling in the empty pews,
wearing their green God-given uniforms,
putting up with every footstep
and unheeding animal trotting across their sweet faces.

Summer Cancan

A summer evening,
a grove of maple trees.
The wind lifts their green dresses,
revealing moss-white underthings,
girls kicking their legs,
doing the cancan,
frothy white slips and petticoats.

During the dance,
I hear the coo of mourning doves,
scolding squirrels,
and loud country music
from a neighbor's house.

Echoing across
the maple-quiet evening,
it's getting dark and cool
and summer is slipping away,
like Josephine Baker
blowing
goodbye kisses
at the stage door.

Strange Beauty

I found two dead groundhogs
in the road,
mother and baby.
I moved them away from traffic
with a stick.

First,
the roly-poly mommy,
a slight head injury
as if asleep,
black paws like hands raised up
as she rolled,
like a soft, sweet dance.
Her mottled fur,
browns and blacks.
Lovely.
I rolled her like a child
down a little hill.

Her baby,
quite another thing.
Half her size, disemboweled.
I rolled him over too,
his intestines trailed out.
"Poor thing."

Rolling his body,
the bright green of summer leaves
just eaten
stood out against his innards,
revealing a strange beauty:
the perfection of his body.

Impromptu Dissection

Once, the plumber killed a black snake.
Angry at the plumber
and sorry for the snake,
we studied it for Science.
We opened its glossy
elongated mystery
without a chart.
Four kids and me,
like a Gary Larson cartoon.
But then we saw
four
maybe five
baby birds
in the long digestive tomb.
We met two
handmaidens of research:
fascination and sorrow.

Stoplight

At a stoplight
a hawk flew over
the hood of my car.
Swinging from her talons—
a tiny mouse.
I breathed a prayer of pity.
From atop a street lamp
little brown shreds floated down
as the light turned green.

Emotional Yogurt

Blueberries, yogurt, granola.
You sit and stare like a Raja.
You touch my hand with your paw,
I stroke your head, chin, and jaw.
If I give you yogurt in a dish
beside your kibbled tuna fish
you ignore it.
But on my fingertip,
you explore it.
I know my breakfast looks divine.
You don't want yours, you want mine.

The Last Morsel

As has been our long-time tradition
I leave the last bite for you.
As I finish a meal,
I look for you,
loving how you lean
against my leg
with sincere eyes,
and the slow saliva drip
collecting by your paws on the floor
until I give you,
by decree,
the last morsel.

The Fifth Valve

We're all so wounded
I'm amazed any of us can breathe.
There's a basement
at the bottom
of a thousand steps,
where there's an old valve as big as a steering wheel,
and you need both hands to open it,
because in most of us
it's rusted shut.

The litanies and laundry lists
of merciless teasing,
harsh parenting,
posturing bosses,
shallow friendships,
fear of failure,
lying to others,
lying to ourselves,
the mean words,
short tempers,
hard hearts,
self-justifications,
manipulations,
defense mechanisms,
and coping strategies,
numb us into distortions
of our real selves.

So one day,
when the death feelings are looming
and the hot tears are searing,
you run down those steps
and you wrestle
and kick that valve
until it opens,
because the love reservoir
has been there all along.
You just needed to be
desperate enough
to open it.

The Green Wheel

Science fiction shows have too much metal.
I'd die in a spaceship.
Give me
green spacious canopies of trees
sunlit new-green leaves
delicate young-green shoots
pine-needle-green northern forests
heat-soaked green jungles
foot-soft green moss
fragrant sun-soaked grass
cool-green branches overhead.

I want to live
in the green wheel,
where the heart spirals outward,
huge,
like a galaxy.

I Don't Want
to Miss a Moment

I so often see myself
as a little boat
on a raging sea.
So much so,
that when the sea is calm
my eyes are still shut tight.

I fail to see the bosom pink of the sunrise,
the robin's egg curve of the silvery sky.
I can't feel the breath of the morning
because I'm squeezing the railings
of my life too hard.

Let me remember the simplicity of beauty.
Once I wasn't here.
Someday,
I'll be gone.

Let me see this life
with my eyes open today.

I don't want to miss a moment
by a mind
tangled in worry.

Let the chirping birds consecrate this morning.
I kneel at their altar and listen to their hymns.

Song of Seeds and Dirt

I read somewhere
when seeds are planted
their devas
sing them
special songs

song of kale
song of cabbage
morning songs
like mothers singing

plump seeds
yawn
awaken
and uncurl
in the glory
of delicious
dirt

by august
walking onions
have walked to the moon
tomatoes are a jungle tangle

green upon green upon green

happy worms
happy slugs
happy dirt

everything
singing

Bug City

From my open window in the dark
I hear them leaving messages
The ringing of bug telephones
And pagers and other images

My screens keep out low-flying planes
The throbbing clicking buzzers sound
That buzz and crash and try again
As insects call and make the rounds

The whippoorwill and bobwhite call
The owl the bat the cricket song
The wings the legs the voices all
Join the cacophonous sing-along

The spring peepers lay awake and cheep
Cicadas rub their legs to death
Mosquitoes buzz quite near our ears
Attracted by our sleepy breath

Daytime the bugs aren't obvious
They do their buggy best all day
When I lie in bed to sleep
Is when they're loudest, when they play

I don't like spider's mandibles
Don't like the hornet's stinger
Don't like mosquitoes' noses much
Don't want to be their dinner

[lyrics looking for a tune]

The Scent of a Ladybug

Really? I said. They have a scent?
Yes, said my son,
they smell sort of like fireflies.
Who could imagine that?
The windowsill of his room
was a gridlock of marching ladybugs,
with more on the floor.
I saved two from drowning in a glass of water—
well, one was dead.
The stillness of her legs,
of the orange-shellac shell with yellow spots—
a style still all the rage.
Very hip, very mod.
But in a week or so,
the bodies were piled
like a Volkswagen scrapyard.
I had no idea they have a scent.
Of course,
everyone knows
the scent of fireflies.

Medevac Bee

Honeybee on blacktop,
turning circles in the heat.
I medevacked him to a bush
with a stretcher of receipt.
He clung there in the shade,
to life and to leaf.
Sent up a prayer for bee,
his people; their relief.

Ground of Being

I set my soles on the ground of being,
my soul on the ground of Your Being.
Wherever thou goest I wish to go.
Whichever way the world tilts,
with You
I wish to be.

No matter what slides off the deck
of my sinking ship,
no matter how I fly by centrifugal force
from my imagined course,
You are my rudder.
In shambles or ecstasy
You are my Holy Ground.

I know there is a primal goodness within all things
that ultimately steers us all toward love.
I glimpse sacred moments
that calm the waves of worry
in this
ever
tumultuous
life.

I Tell It to the Gods

I lie on grass and think of fragile earth,
all the tempests in our teacups.
I tell it to the gods.
My sacred planet,
silly planet,
fellow earthlings off their meds,
screaming tantrums,
smashing crockery,
cradling the crying babies.
Earth is like an underworld.
Orpheus, we need a song.

The Last Straw

The secret to the quandary
of the last straw
is forgiveness.
When I want to punch someone's lights out
I don't want to think about that,
but I know it's true.
One more straw
can be very light
if I untie the bundle
and let
them
all
blow
away.

Prayer Is a Convertible

God told me,
put the top down
on your gloomy outlook.

Prayer is a convertible
let the wind blow your hair crazy
let the sun burn your neck and nose
ride baby ride into the sunset
put a sunroof in your soul.

The Fear Before Knocking

Yeah, yeah
I know, I know.
Just knock and it will be opened.
Seek, ask, knock.
If I do
will you stand me up?
Do I open myself to ridicule?
Gullible! Naive! Ignorant!
The fear before knocking
is like showing up for a blind date.
Will I be wanted
or am I the weirdo?
Hence, I resist, my knuckles raised,
yet frozen.

I Don't Want to Be Smote!

I don't want to be smote!
I want to be held by my Daddy.
Is that so wrong?
I'm willing to face hardships.
I've been poor and evicted,
sad and suicidal,
confused and heart-hardened.
I gave up and broke down.
I was ready to fill my pockets with rocks
and go for my last swim.

Then a spring peeper called out
from the warming reeds
in the standing water.
The sweetness of the call
awoke the others,
and in their song
I found another spring
worth living for.

Why Must I Be Emotional?

Why must I be emotional?
I just want to be devotional.
But before I know what happens
I grow fangs.
Then I'm responsible
for being mean and irritable
and then my conscience
reverberates with pangs.

The Attack of Raptors

There are moments in life
that startle us from the side
like the attack of raptors.

We're facing forward
while being devoured—
before our chewed brain
even knows it's being eaten.

The descent
into the digestion
of the event
has happened
before we know
our destiny
has changed.

The digestive juice
melts everything we knew.

In denial, we grope
for the rewind button,
for the editing software,
for anything to take us back
to the moment before.

Go back, go back, go back.
But the bridge is blown
and we can't go back
and our limbs are gone
and our eyes are gone
and this is life now.

The cynical side says:
Get used to crawling.
But the God within
knows there's a way out.

Our Dumb Adult Tea Party

If we could hear
the moaning of the animals confined
in deplorable spaces
without water or food.
If we could hear the moaning of the oceans
choking on plastic.

If we could see ourselves as six-year-olds
in the kitchens of the earth,
turning stove knobs wildly,
mixing anything and everything
into explosive poisons,
serving it all in teacups
at our tea party,
in our big dumb adult bodies,
our hearts unplugged from
the heartbeat of the earth.

Then epiphanies might rain down,
waking us from our stupor.

David and His Grandmother

In the photograph
a white-haired woman
and a young man
face the camera,
their arms around each other's waists.
It's a crowd shot
but they stand out.

We pose in pictures
forcing smiles
sometimes with those we do not love.
We look later
and wonder.
Where?
Who?

But these two!

Have real affection.
Joy in their connection!
I wish I had a grandma
or an auntie
whose beautiful wrinkles I could love
whose eyes I could smile into.

Atonal City

New York.
Gulag gray buildings,
Sidewalks and subway steps
serving millions of feet,
germ-dancing railings,
everyone coping,
averting eyes,
en route.

Sparrows find gutter crumbs,
a piano scale from a window,
the shrieking of car horns.

Incessant processing,
a giant body,
enzymes and blood cells,
girders and garbage,
glass and grime,
a relentless,
atonal
song.

La La Land

People talk about being in La La Land.
You go there when you're stupid
or clueless.
You're there when you're naive
or ignorant.
People get enraged when you go there.
But you never remember going.
They scream at you,
but you don't remember it.
Do they have a beach and a boardwalk?
Do they sell lemonade and cotton candy?
Nothing on the credit card statement.
No receipts.
I wish they'd stamp your hand
or something when you go there,
so you'd have some proof.
A screaming photo from a roller coaster
would do.
But all you have is a kind of amnesia.
And angry people
screaming your name.

What Really Happened?

To look at something
anything
to see it
means
really looking.

There's a timeline
the history of it all
what people tell themselves
what other people witness
or assume.

Why is truth so interchangeable?
I thought it was one thing,
but
what really happened?

Black Box

After a crash,
they search for the black box.
It contains the hows and whys.
I wish we could locate
each person's black box.
Analysis could take a lifetime.

Data on strands of DNA,
ticker tapes of rage and blame,
everybody's hows and whys,
dating back to the Big Bang.

HEY!
Where's that black box?
All our en masse reasons
for why and who we are
are stuffed into it.
No one knows where it is.
Maybe hidden
with the Holy Grail.

The Forensics of Violence

What if they call a lamp to the witness stand?
Or a sofa?
Or a rug?
The ones who watched the violence.
Sitting in it, under it, next to it,
affected by it.
They saw it all.

They know who did what
to who
and when.
And how.

They had to hold their breath
and stay still.

When a glass on a table
draws
attention
to itself—
if it gulps—
it gets thrown against the wall.

Beads of sweat
form
on the foreheads of bottles,
vases,
and lamps.
They know
they're getting it next.

When you enter a room
after
violence,
all witnesses
carry
the story.
It orbits in their molecules.

Archaeologists
dust off
broken crockery
to preserve the beauty,
but does anyone heal the wounds?

Does anyone hear their story?

Gathering Storm

I don't remember in my lifetime
such a sense of gathering storm
that seems to swell around
our dear earth.
Blood hot anger,
deprivations squeezing.
Have the graves of the past
even decomposed?
Myriads of the dead
gather and look
through the glass
holding their breath.
Wondering.
Will we do any better?

Gored by the Bull of Love

My heart is as dry as a desert
with a cactus of love in my soul
Our love terrain
is like the middle of Spain
eroded as the famous Dust Bowl

In the center of Spain is a bullring
like the ring that's upon my hand
where the dance of pikes and pujas
spill irreparable blood on the sand

This toreador suit was expensive
You're snortin' hot from the sunshine above
The swords of pain have set you a bleedin'
but I've been gored by the bull of love

Darlin', what can put an end to this heartbreak?
I can't keep dancin' with a red cape all day
Your hoof stamps the dirt
I wipe my face with your shirt
and we both collapse on the clay

[lyrics looking for a tune]

Multitudinous Fray

Sparrows are brawling in the holly bush,
a Shakespearean fray
of noise and flapping.
A beak fight in the birdie saloon!
Birdies of the evening flirt from branchy lounges,
while the birdy fellers duke it out,
scuffling and swaggering,
pecking everything in sight.
A generous birdtender
calms the throng
as passions dwindle.
"A round of seeds for everyone!" he chirps.
"All's well that ends well."

October Day

Traipsing along copper paths,
in star-topped strands of grass,
with my doe-colored dog,

butterflies hovered in
purple flowers as I
looked down
into a pond
and saw
a gathering of
bright-faced cattails.

Brown and tall,
they looked eagerly at me,
like children
awaiting the recess bell—
so well dressed
and dear
in matching
brown pullovers.

Nature gives
her best
so very quietly.

Can a Month Be Grumpy?

Today could be January 32nd.
If it was, who would notice?
The people born on February 1st?
February would just have to shove over a little,
or maybe lose a day.
A twenty-seven-day month.
It's not a popular month,
it's an extension of the bleak midwinter.
We celebrate Lincoln's
and Washington's birthdays
and Valentine's Day,
but who would really notice
if we changed the dates
except Aquarians and Pisceses
(Good God,
what is the plural of Pisces,
somewhat like the plural
of fish! Is that a coincidence?)

Of course, in the Southern Hemisphere,
it's the hot midsummer, and that changes
everything.
The only thing to do is to
change the page of the calendar on my wall
and act as if it's all going as planned.
But what if the whole year was just
ONE LONG JANUARY?
January 150th?
January 300th?

It makes the brain spin.
And even talking about it
makes the other months
grumpy—
can't you feel it?

The Sugar Maple

The sugar maple
is bathed in sun.

Her autumn leaves
make ready and leap.

I watch them pass my window,
streaks of yellow,
like tiny falling stars.

The Pen and Ink Sky

In winter, the dawn sky
looks like pen and ink,
the black trees in all their
thicknesses and webbing,
the wash of translucent gray
carries colorless light,
which seems to emerge
from the ground.

Night Prayer

My voice is swallowed by the woods
as I sing into the dark
my boots make pathways as I walk
the stars begin to spark.
Rosy grays and rosy blues
waft and wash the milky skies
the creaking trees clack hard as bones
as the moon begins to rise.

Crows

I didn't mean to scare the crows away.
I heard metallic voices,
saw the shadow of their wings.
I knew what it meant then
to see through a glass darkly.

They came for seeds.
I was glad they came to feed,
but when I appeared in the window,
they fled.

They seem so fierce with
their bone beaks
and their tar-black feathers
and their abrasive caws,
but I would love to feed one from my hand.

Black Lucy

In the bathroom
while reading a magazine
I hear hoofbeats
beyond the drawn curtain.

I peep outside at the paddock
across the road,
and see
Black Lucy galloping
in the freezing rain.
Gorgeous and Wet and
Galloping.

Dreams of a Fruit Fly

How simple and sweet
the dreams of the fruit fly
beguiled awake by
a corpsey black banana.
And lured thus,
joins its fellows
in a dance of the sugarplum fruit flies,
having no itinerary,
no agenda,
no fact-finding mission,
just flitting over fetid fruit,
drunk in feast and fragrance,
a merry orbiting
above a trash can
in a corner of neglect.

Raccoon Interrupted

In the center of the road
lies a mangled raccoon.
Right on the yellow line,
disemboweled,
the sweet face intact,
looking at my headlights
in shock.
The striped tail laid straight out,
the soft peaked ears,
sooty mask.
But his middle crushed.
So sorry for an innocent life
who was just out looking for dinner.

The Sorghum Cows

Last Saturday
I drove home through Sorghum.
The flaky Virginia January
was like a muggy summer day.
The Sorghum cows chewed
and sprawled on the grass
like a day at the beach.

Seven days later,
it's now below freezing
and snowing.

The cows stand stunned
and snow trimmed,
like tractors and trees.

They stand still,
not moving, not mooing,
like ceramic knickknack cows.
Not blinking
not eating
on a cold ceramic hillside
enduring the weather
with nowhere to go.

Whistler's Mother

If you put Whistler's Mother
in a pair of jeans and work boots
and pull her gray hair into a ponytail,
she might look like any ol' gal at the farmer's market.

Bonnets and black dresses didn't do any favors
for young hearts in old bodies.
Who knows?
Whistler's Mother may have longed for a contra dance
instead of being
confined to a wooden chair for eternity.

Her feet may have longed for a twirl around the room,
her white handkerchief
dabbing tears away
between brushstrokes
that obscured
her long-abandoned dreams.

Love Is a Strange Address

From the beer-soaked glare of a blaring TV bar
dreams that never got a chance to land
in the wooded, fearful fog
of a pounding longing heart,
that forgot the words of its inner song.

Love is a strange address.

Prayers uttered in the chapel of the soul
question marks suspended in the
waiting room of love,
when will the love of
consequence arrive
in a place without numbers on the door.

Love is a strange address.

[lyrics looking for a tune]

Soul Resonance

Once on vacation when I was little
I met a girl in the pool,
and we played all day.
We became friends the way kids do.
We laughed at jokes,
played on the slide,
and jumped in the water.
Soul resonance.

We promised to meet at the pool
the next day
to say goodbye,
exchange addresses,
and become pen pals.

My family left early in the morning.
I begged my parents
but I could not go to the pool
to say goodbye to my new friend.

I cried all the way home.

I've always been like that.
When the frequency of my soul
touches the frequency of another
I can't let go of the thread.

I still want to press my forehead
against her forehead
and say
I remember you.

The Makeover

I keep attempting a makeover.
But not the external kind with paints and potions.
I secretly feel too far-gone for those.
My hair isn't interested,
then there's all that flab,
and frankly,
I have no interest in polish or fashion.

Unless I could be a cowgirl again.
I like the idea of a fringe jacket
and a well-made cowboy hat
that just suits me,
and some dandy boots,
not to mention
the dark-eyed horse of my dreams.
A wild gallop sounds tempting,
even though I never learned to ride . . .

But the makeover!
It would involve a shake-up,
with good habits that stick,
shedding the husks of "normal"
that have posed as a life.

I welcome the kind of makeover
that shines out from the core
like a ripening peach
in the light of a dawning day.

Menopause

Standing on my steps with a
glass of wine,
looking down on the fading light
over the woods
below the smudge of night,
I think
what a lovely day.

Somewhere, moose are rutting.
The males drop weight in the fall,
their minds occupied with finding a female.
They can't
they don't
eat.
You can't distract
the primal urge.

The Holstein cows in the far field
crowd around their bale.
No males disrupt their dinner
with acts of passion,
or pining feelings, but
I am pining.

I cannot name the feeling at workday's end.
The kettle boiling,
the chicken frying.
"The young-uns growed and moved on . . ."
I sip my wine
and watch
the sweet crackling autumn evening
burn over the hill,
and feel the yellow glow
in my solar plexus,
remembering
days of heat.

Transmogrified

One day,
I noticed
that life was moving
at an odd pace.

I was sixty,
arthritic, and limping.
My youth and sexual energy
had transmogrified
into a low-grade pulse
of love for all things.

Where is my place in all this?
Hell if I know.
I just know I'm still here,
trying to do my best.

Cleaning

Soap in the bucket
Grime in the dregs
Centipede kicking
suds from his legs
Streaks on the walls
Dirt on the floor
Scrub them stains
and prints off the door

Beginnings Without Fizzle

If I had a dollar for all my beginnings . . .

New exercise regimen.
New eating habits.
New determinations
with marital dynamics,
writing,
and budgeting.

Oy.

The funny thing about these
bold beginnings
is they often fizzle.
They don't end.
They fade away.

Nature's beginnings are robust!
The zygote, the hatchling, the bud!
Once set in motion,
they don't forget what they're doing.
They become!

I pray for follow-through
so my beginnings don't end
puny, dead on arrival, kaput,
but unfold to fruition.

May I put an end to fizzle!

Self Portrait

People pleaser,
enabler,
co-dependent.

Courageous,
independent,
rebellious.

Angry,
greedy,
irritable.

Tender-hearted,
generous,
cooperative.

Is the jagged jigsaw
a fait accompli?

Perhaps
prayers,
dreams,
actions
alter
destiny.

Shelter

I've been searching for home.
Living in so many places
all my life
I have no roots.

The nomad gene.
So pervasive.
No place fits for long.

I have a shelter in my heart
with a shining sun
and a place to sit.

Wherever I am,
if I'm lost and alone,
I retreat there.

Mrs. Lot

I try to live in the present.
I'm punctual.
I only have today.
The future is a rumor,
like passing myself on the highway.
A mirage
that never comes,
until I look back
and I'm salt.

Look Both Ways

I do!
That's my problem.
Too many possibilities,
like Tevye:
"On the other hand . . ."
Second-guessing,
can't decide.
God, grant me the serenity
to make up my mind.

The Old Black Dogs

The old black dogs howl at my throat.
Nothing means anything.
Nothing is sacred.

My secret "Ways to Commit Suicide" list
gleefully shrieks to me:
Do it this way!
No, this way!
They'll be sorry!

I throw a juicy bone of regret,
and with a frenzied dash
they pounce and gnaw on it.

Somehow I face the new day.

Antenna Gut

I pick up feelings
like TV signals.
They permeate
like barbecue smoke
in a closed room.
They go into my gut
and settle like E. coli
in a takeout curry dinner.

Sometimes the shakes,
sometimes nausea.

There's a News Guy who shows up
with a bow tie
and a voice like Walter Winchell
pelting questions,
digging for dirt,
spreading rumors,
telling lies,
letting in the throng.

The copper plates of justice swing
in my cranial hemispheres:

Oh, they have a point.
And
so do they.

The tirade rattles and cajoles
like a cloud of roosting crows.
A din.
Like tinnitus with
nowhere to go.

A Voyage

The HMS Zygote sailed one night,
launched from a gleam in my Father's eye.

Since then
my innocence has stood the test
of life's laboratories,
dissected and dipped in caustic solutions,
hung up to dry while flies landed.

On the other hand,
the gaze of loving eyes
and a thousand other joys
on this journey
allow me to say in all sincerity:

Glorioski, ain't life grand?

Ancestral Spirals

Looking at the spiral of hair
on the back of my little boy's head,
I wonder about the hair
on the backs of the heads
of all the little boys
in my lineage.

Boys hugged by their mothers,
boys unsure of themselves
who grew up to be men,
who were unsure of themselves,
who fathered more boys.

I see the likeness in them,
the similarities.
I want to help straighten
our ancestry
from its skewed axis,
as I stroke my little boy's head,
fingering the swirl of his hair,
and the mystery of our DNA . . .
helix
spiral
coral
ringlets
pine cone
tornado
spiral of generations.

Rain Dance

Weeks of blasting heat
then,
blessed thunderstorm!
While the stomachs of the sky people rumble
the girl and boys streak out to the driveway
to dance
a fairy dance,
kicking up their heels like joyous goats,
the pummeling rain
washing over them as they squeal
and the pavement steams.

The Best Moment

I love the moment
when
Bewildered
meets
Cognition.

The best moment
is when you and I
are wrangled in a bear trap
of hurt and rage,
entombed in silent casings,
or blowing fire like unleashed banshees,
and then . . .

A little
cog
clicks
into
place
like the sun
emerging
from a tempest.

And I get you.
And you get me.
A drum roll!
A cymbal!
A tiny hooray
for humanity!

Newspapers

When I was a child,
I thought the word
obituary
was a swear word,
because it had
the word
bitch
in it.

But if I whispered
"obituary!"
under my breath
I wasn't swearing.

After I was told
that the word meant
death announcements
I wondered
how they got
the dead people to smile
for the photos.

Speaking of newspapers,
back then
we got the New York Times.
On Sundays,
my Dad
brought the whole thing
into the bathroom.

So, you better not have to go.

2 A.M.

The hurricane is stalled off the coast.
You're at your desk working.
I wake up burdened with worries.
I see your lamp,
the sight of you cheers me.
I make us tea.
A fly drowns in yours
and you almost drink it
until I warn you.
We laugh.
I make you another.
I watch an old movie about love.
It lifts my burdens.
I go back to bed before dawn.
You keep working.
The children sleep.
The wind howls outside.
We have love.

The CEO

I thought you were worthy
I contorted myself for you
I emptied myself of personal desire
to accommodate you.
There were inappropriate boundaries,
you never wondered how I felt.
I let it happen.
I let it happen.
I let it happen.
I want your apology.
I'll never get it.
What I did get
was a shred of self-respect
which I found,
with my guts,
when I left.

A Small Insult

A small insult
a small comment
enters me like an arrow
stinging my heart.
First, I want to hit back—
then I find my heart again
and cry.
This is PUNY.
Teach me your heart, God.
Teach me to accept what comes
and ever cling to your love.

Current Events

Once, I thought, I'll write a memoir!
Show my innocence and their guilt.
But Revenge is the Lowest Rung.
Condemnation, the Lowest Vibration.

When I think you're guilty,
what does that make me?
An authority? Someone better?
Retribution is a dead end.
A collapsed lung.
A withered heart.
Necrosis of the soul.

Forgive them.
They know not what they did.
Forgive me,
I know not what I did.
We live in the Eternal NOW.
Not the eternal THEN.
Whatever happened is over.
What about from now?

We are swatches from the same cloth.
The dark meanderings
of human stupidity, human cruelty,
could have been you,
could have been me.
Some insist on delineation, but
I submit that the image we project reflects back.

Forgiveness
is the lifeline.
The way out
from the descending
corkscrew
of
accusations.

Forgiveness is an oxygen tank.
Forgiveness is a blood transfusion.
Smoke forgiveness in a pipe.
Spread forgiveness on toast.
Forgiveness, lettuce, and tomato.
Forgiveness baked in a pie.
Forgiveness on the rocks.
Forgiveness à la mode.
Until my pores sweat it.
My eyes shine it.
My heart thumps it.
My life lives it.

I Am One of Them

I can hardly see.
I am one of them,
with log-heavy eyes
pointing out specks.

Teach me to walk a mile
in Italian leather,
in stilettos,
with burning calloused soles,
with shoeless feet.

See from penthouse windows,
from filthy tarp flaps.

I am among what I call "Other."
Yet, I am from you,
with you, am you.

Ensouled from the beginning
in the moist, tingling honesty
of cosmic placenta.
There is no "Other."

Even at the Call Center

Even here,
even here among the headphones
and the keyboards
You are here.

My soul, Your soul, and the souls of others,
converging in this dry room, of indoor/outdoor carpeting,
overhead fluorescent light, computer screens, and telephones—
You are here.

Somehow the soulless materials have soul because
everything comes from You.
It is immensely comforting,
immensely comforting to me
that even in a synthetic environment,
the green pulse of Your heart is here.

The Mention of Your Name

Some people have a visceral reaction
at the mention of your name.
God.
Some say you are out there,
some say you are nowhere,
but I know you're "in here,"
in mucous, blood, and semen,
growls, guts, guttural sounds.
In blazing summer sun,
merciless winter wind,
yellow baby poo,
and old people's toothless gums.

You are the primal core
of love and mercy,
of kindness.
Green pastures and starry skies
dispel our fear a little.
But what we really want is
Your enormous Mother's Heart,
to leak milk from a huge, soft tit
and feed us; the starving world.

Your Father's heart
was presented
like a dry knuckle
in our starving mouths.
People of Earth are posturing,
attempting to be cool,
when we are actually shivering
weenies
longing for a reassuring hug
and milk and cookies
on the cosmic kitchen table.

Broke

The last square of toilet paper
The last Cheerio
The last bean
The check's in the mail.

Overdrawn

Overdrawn, overdrawn
Ain't got nothin' left to pawn
When will we have enough to live on?
Overdrawn.

Death and taxes death and taxes
Living on the tilted axis
Credit cards and bills are maxed out
Overdrawn

Someday we'll have enough to buy
The basic stuff to live and die
You wonder how you wonder why
Overdrawn

Tomorrow the sun will shine
Tomorrow the rain will fall
In a couple of years
Our debts will be
Forgotten like the Neanderthal

[lyrics looking for a tune]

Monster

To be a monster
you need a lair,
crazy eyes
and sticky hair.
An unhinged mind,
unblinking stare.
Effective monsters
like to lurk
and wait for folks
come home from work.
Monsters like
the sight of blood
and dragging victims
through the mud.
No one taught them how to play
or right from wrong
or how to pray.
They spend their youth
in school detention.
Toothless, old,
they get no pension.

Machine

Cavemen hunted all day long
which kept them strong and tough.
Cave ladies never shaved their legs
Their skin was always rough.
Modern men go to the gym
and use all their machinery.
Modern ladies go there too.
They both enjoy the scenery.

Fishing for Poems

There are cracks between dimensions
where you can pull poems through.
They hang like stars in an unseen sky.
When a heart
fishes
for a word
wanting
to name a thought,
they can't help
swimming through.
If you catch them,
you have to hold them
while
they thrash
and fill you with a feeling.
Then take out
the hook,
pat their glossy scales,
and let them
disappear.
But find your pen first.

Have Mercy

Lay off his temperature settings.
Don't worry about soup wasted down the drain.
What about the fact
that he's got my back?
I know if he wasn't here
it would feel like the great North Wind
blowing through my soul.

The heat of his heart is kind.
Supportive love.

There's something about "acceptance."
You accept what is, "who is," and
there's no expectation anymore.

I'm glad to see
His faithful, loving face.

Outposts of Love

We have not yet reached the outposts of love.
We're in those between days,
sorta kinda sixty old,
but not cataract-crippled mind-blank ninety-nine old.
So in this interim,
even though we still behave like toddlers
whining and crying for our own way sometimes,
I still love the shuffle of your slippers slapping
through the house,
your loud conversations on speakerphone with
god knows who,
the reheating of the tea kettle till it burns itself out.

Those are signs of You Here.
You always say good morning,
hello, goodbye,
please and thank you,
You call me when it doesn't seem necessary,
but all of these things make a life.
If they're ever gone from me
I want you to at least know
that I noticed it all,
was grateful for it all,
and recognized it for the beauty
I could so easily overlook,
but kissed to my heart, each day.

A Shamrock in the Snow
for My Brother

A date on the calendar.
Your birthday.
My heart squeezes when I see it,
February 6th,
leaving my soul bereft
for the you I never knew.

I will light a candle on your day,
I will find a shamrock in the February snow,
I will share Air with you, eat cake,
and see something of your face
in the face of my son.

Tymon Is Born

You were born early.
Daddy drove to Washington, DC
because you weren't due yet.
We said goodbye.

I felt a nesting urge.
I cleaned bookcases.
I washed laundry.

I did not know then
that I would wake at 6 a.m.,
soaking the sheets
when my water broke,
announcing
your imminent
arrival
in the
world.

I called Julie Andrews.
Yes,
our doula's name.
She was asleep.
She said,
don't worry,
go back to sleep.
I said,
GO BACK TO SLEEP?
I was terrified.
No labor pains yet.

Your daddy was working
alone in an office.
No one else was there
because it was Saturday.

I couldn't reach him.
This was before cell phones.
Imagine what a stone age it was.
I called his boss at home.
The boss had to drive to the building
to find your daddy.

Go home.
Your wife is in labor.

I drove myself to the hospital.
I stopped at a gas station.
I just had to tell someone,

Hey, I'm going to have a baby today,
I'm driving to the hospital.

There was nobody else to tell.

When I got there about noon,
they hooked me up to Pitocin
and the contractions started.

Your daddy arrived and
although I don't remember it,

held my hand
and was with me
the whole time.

I didn't intend to have any drugs.
I didn't know what pain was.
When I learned what pain was,
they gave me an epidural and I slept.

The next morning,
I remember seeing the
shiny flash of forceps
and seeing a
man in scrubs and a mask
leaning on the wall
and saying to whoever was
listening,
Who is that guy?
It was daddy.

They told me to push.
Finally, you were born.

It was a Sunday morning.
It was the first real Sabbath of my life.
You were the first child,
and the realization of my baby boy in my arms
was the morning and evening of the first day,
the Genesis of my existence.
I met what LOVE was and is
and I have never been the same.

Beer and Pizza and a Hug

Looking at the shaved head
the red beard
the brown knitted watch cap
the height of your lean body
the red checkered shirt
the brown Dickey trousers and vest
the water-proof Rockport shoes
your gray-blue eyes.

We connected today
as never before.
Tears fell
when I knew
really knew
my child loves me
and I love him.
And more,
he understands me,
and I hope I do him.

I felt the hum and purr
of understanding
conveyed
during
beer and pizza
and a big hug
under the darkening
October sky in Portland.

Goob

When you were a baby
you had one big curl
on top of your head
the foreshadowing
of the storm of curls
you have now

I want to go back
to when you were tiny
I want to carry you around

I want to listen
to you
learning
to talk

I want to look at your
sweet self
for hours

You unfolded before me

A woman

Intelligent
funny
warm
beautiful
and brave

Such an honor
to have known you
from the beginning

What a lucky mother
that you came to me
that you
are
my daughter

Fen and Iris

There are very few people
in my life now
who knew my parents.
It is wonderful to me
that someone I know
heard the voices and saw
the faces of Fen and Iris.
Maybe you don't remember
them as I do,
but they hold a time for me.
The welcoming kindness of my mother.
The obtuse, confusing humor of my father.
Even back then,
everyone who visited
left our house
covered in dog hair.

A tradition I will carry on into perpetuity.

At the Hour
of Our Death, Amen

At the hour of our death, amen,
does our life play like a video?
All the standout moments;
the blood splash and cry of birth,
significant birthdays, applause, and cake?
Traumas and yearnings,
confusions and burnings,
elations of love?

Can we see the reasons why,
like the wiring and plumbing hidden in walls,
that led us to this sorrow or that joy?
Does a voice we know narrate our story,
comforting the stupid and shameful moments,
encouraging the times we were brave?

In the arc of our life,
from sperm/egg explosion
to final death rattle—
how great it would be to know
that the underpinnings of love
were all there in the journey,
that when we turn the garment
of our life inside out
they show up like careful, fine stitches.

Thank You
for the Mysteries

Thank you for the mysteries
of secret
realms
where love
glistens
and heals
nourishes
and transforms
with ineffable filters

the charcoal of worry
the sludge of cruelty
the anvil of self-doubt

where they are
aerated
into floating microscopic
water droplets
of the love
of heaven
and spray like
stars
into the vast oceans of
space.

The Eternal Now

The eternal now
is always here
even
if we do things
one at a time.

My Will

Finance, real estate, credit score, 401(k)
are all at zero.

But I bank at the Bank of Love.
I try to make daily deposits
and God knows I've withdrawn sums all my life.
I've received love with interest!

And I'm interested in love.

I hope to deposit pocketfuls
and mountains of love.

At the end, I write my will:

I bequeath my enormous fortune of love to the entire universe
from whence it came.

I hope my inheritors cash it in and throw a huge party.

Everyone's invited!

Wagging

More than anything, I hope
that I can boil down to the essence
of a happy, wagging dog.
Just glad to see everybody.

If dementia sets in,
let that be my default setting.

I may not know who the hell you are
but I just want to wag and smile,
and love you.

Love everybody.
Love anybody.
Just because you exist.

If all my opinions and habits and preferences
end up in a vault
with a question mark on the label,
and no one is left who even knows my name,

the one thing I hope I have left
is the impulse to love,
to wag like a happy dog
until I roll over
and play dead for real.

About the Author

Kimmy Sophia Brown was born in upstate New York and spent her formative childhood years in the small, farming community of Cassville, where she learned about the beauty of animals and nature.

After that, she moved to Chicago and experienced "city shock." But she survived and returned to the East Coast in 1970 where she went to high school. Later, she worked briefly as a welder in a submarine shipyard in Connecticut and then backpacked and hitchhiked (it was the '70s) around Europe for a few months.

As an adult, she traveled to California and back again, experiencing life in dozens of states along the way.

She and her husband, Peter, raised four lovely children in Virginia, and survived that too, even though they were transplanted Yankees.

Now, she lives in the countryside of Maine. Although it's not Cassville, there are birds and coyotes, cows and horses, dogs and cats, and farmers with mud on their boots. Also, there's that great little bonus of the Atlantic Ocean right up the road.

She feels right at home.

You may read her works at her website, kimmysophiabrown.com, or contact her via email at kimbrown@worldcommunity.com.

Notes

These notes include sources on two quotes as well as dedications of poems to various persons or animals. They also include notations if they are "Lyrics in Search of a Tune." If you're a musician and you want to put them to music, email me at kimbrown@worldcommunity.com. Finally, there are some source notes, etc.

Quotes:

1. *A Course in Miracles, Combined Volume*, Second Edition, Chapter 1, "The Meaning of Miracles," Section 1, "Principles of Miracles," Verse 3, (Mill Valley, CA, Foundation for Inner Peace, 1992), 3.

2. Saint Teresa of Avila, "The Book of Her Life," Chapter 22, Verse 14, in *Saint Teresa of Avila: Collected Works*, trans. Kieran Kavanaugh, O.C.D. and Otilio Rodriguez, O.C.D, (Washington, ICS Publications, 1976), 198.

Poems:

Eclipse: for Surya

There's a Dream in My Bed: for Tadin

Prior to the Cold River Plunge Fully Clothed:
    In 1983 I was working at a summer camp.

Santa Cruz 1973: for Genevieve, Beth, and Karen

After the Farm: Lyrics

Full Moon Cat: for Vinny

Driving a Truck: In 1985, I volunteered for a nonprofit and drove a box truck.

Tiny Boy in July: for Ranin

Six-Week-Old Boy: for Tadin

Mammals' Motherhood: for Tymon and Gracie

Kids On the Lawn: for Tymon, Gracie, Ranin, and Tadin

Kitchen Billiards: When we were young.

Spooky Action: for Rena, Mark, Matthew, Jason, and Devin, 2016 reunion.

1. Karl Tate, "How Quantum Entanglement Works (Infographic)," *Live Science*, April 08, 2013, https://www.livescience.com/28550-how-quantum-entanglement-works-infographic.html

Bug City: Lyrics, 1986

The Scent of a Ladybug: inspired by Ranin

David and His Grandmother:
    Looking at a friend's family photograph from 1986.

Gored by the Bull of Love: Lyrics

Night Prayer: Walking in the woods one night in 1983.

Love Is a Strange Address: Lyrics

Ancestral Spirals: inspired by Ranin's cowlicks

Rain Dance: for Tymon, Gracie, Ranin, and Tadin

Overdrawn: Lyrics, 1995

A Shamrock in the Snow for My Brother: for Dutch

Beer and Pizza and a Hug: for Tadin

Goob: for Grace

Made in the USA
Middletown, DE
04 October 2023

40158995R00135